Mount Everest

Nancy Dickmann

Raintree

Chicago, Illinois

www.capstonepub.com
Visit our website to find out
more information about
Heinemann-Raintree books.

To order:

☎ Phone 800-747-4992

💻 Visit www.capstonepub.com
to browse our catalog and order online.

Edited by Rebecca Rissman, Dan Nunn, and
    Catherine Veitch
Designed by Cynthia Della-Rovere
Leveling by Jeanne Clidas
Picture research by Elizabeth Alexander
Production by Victoria Fitzgerald
Originated by Capstone Global Library
Printed and bound in China by CTPS

16 15 14 13 12
10 9 8 7 6 5 4 3 2 1

**Library of Congress Cataloging-in-Publication
Data**

Dickmann, Nancy.
  Mount Everest / Nancy Dickmann.—1st ed.
    p. cm.—(Explorer tales)
  Includes bibliographical references and index.
  ISBN 978-1-4109-4783-3 (hb)—ISBN 978-1-4109-
4790-1 (pb) 1. Mountaineering—Everest, Mount
(China and Nepal)—History—Juvenile literature. 2. Ever-
est, Mount (China and Nepal)—Discovery and explora-
tion—Juvenile literature. I. Title.
  GV199.44.E85D54 2012
  796.522095496—dc23   2011041473

Acknowledgments
We would like to thank the following for permission
to reproduce photographs: © Royal Geographical
Society p. 16; Alamy pp. 6 (© Image Source), 9
(© Ashley Cooper), 10 (© Pictorial Press Ltd), 13
(© Vintage Image), 14 (© Royal Geographical
Society), 19 (© Ashley Cooper Pics); Corbis pp.
12–13 (© Stefan Chow), 15 (© Stefan Chow), 27
(© Aurora Photos/ Peter McBride); Getty Images
pp. 8 (Jake Norton), 11 (AFP), 17 (Butch Adams/
Stone), 18 (Hulton Archive/ Keystone), 20 (Robert
Harding/ David Pickford), 26 (AFP Photo/ Namgyal
Sherpa), 29 (AFP); Nature Picture Library p. 7 (John
Downer); Press Association Images pp. 21 (AP
Photo/Super Sherpas LLC), 24 (PRESSENS BILD), 25
(BILD/PRESSENS); Reuters p. 22; Rex Features p. 23
(c.Everett Collection); Shutterstock p. 4 (© Ignacio
Salaverria).

Cover photographs of Tenzing Norgay and Edmund
Hillary reproduced with permission of Press
Association Images (AP); map of Asia, c. 1580,
reproduced with permission of Sanders of
Oxford, rare prints & maps (www.sandersofoxford.
com); Top of the World—Mount Everest and Nuptse
reproduced with permission of Shutterstock
(© Momentum). Background image of Mount
Everest reproduced with permission of Shutterstock
(© Ignacio Salaverria).

Every effort has been made to contact copyright
holders of material reproduced in this book. Any
omissions will be rectified in subsequent printings if
notice is given to the publisher.

Disclaimer
All the Internet addresses (URLs) given in this book
were valid at the time of going to press. However,
due to the dynamic nature of the Internet, some
addresses may have changed, or sites may have
changed or ceased to exist since publication. While
the author and publisher regret any inconvenience
this may cause readers, no responsibility for any such
changes can be accepted by either the author or
the publisher.

Contents

The Top of the World 4

Climbing Mount Everest 8

First to the Top? 10

Success at Last 14

Climbing 18

Super Sherpas 20

Crazy Descents 22

Mount Everest by Bike 24

Mount Everest Today 26

Timeline 28

Explorer's Checklist 29

Glossary 30

Find Out More 31

Index 32

Some words are shown in bold, **like this**. You can find out what they mean by looking in the glossary.

The Top of the World

Have you ever wanted to climb a mountain? Mountains tower high above the land, and none is taller than Mount Everest. It is so high and cold that snow covers it all year round.

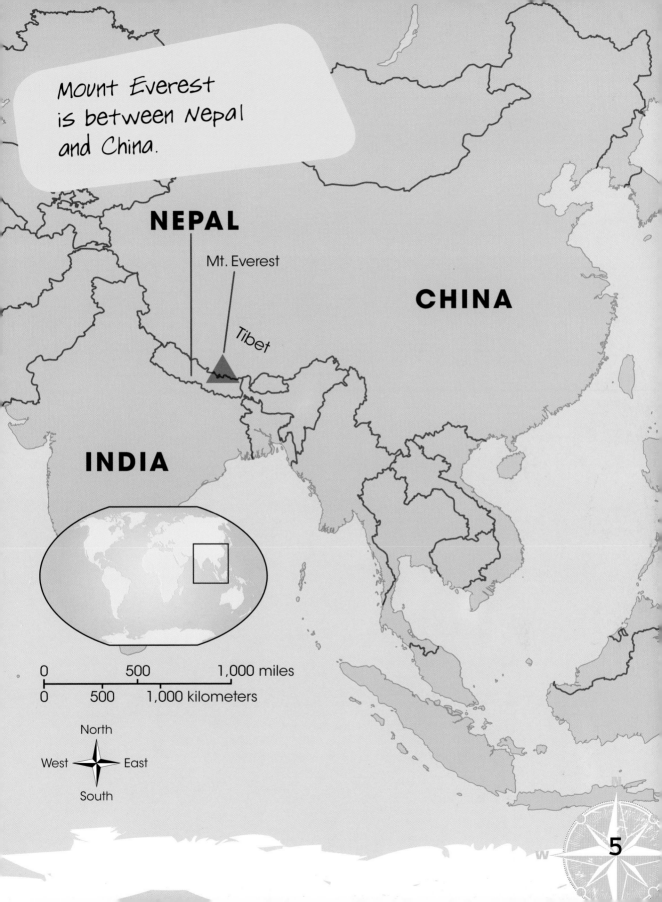

Mount Everest
is between Nepal
and China.

NEPAL

Mt. Everest

Tibet

CHINA

INDIA

0   500   1,000 miles

0   500   1,000 kilometers

North

West   East

South

It is hard to breathe on Everest. At the top there is very little **oxygen** in the air. When climbers do not get enough oxygen, they get headaches, feel sick, and see things that are not really there!

DID YOU KNOW?

The only animals you might see at the top of Mount Everest are bar-headed geese. They fly over the **summit**.

7

Climbing Mount Everest

Climbing Mount Everest seems like a crazy idea. The cold, snow, ice, and falling rocks make it very dangerous. But, thousands of people have tried.

DID YOU KNOW?
For every 19 successful climbs, one climber has died on Mount Everest.

ice ax

Mountain climbers use tools such as ice axes and **crampons** to grip the ice.

crampon

First to the Top?

One morning in 1924, George Mallory and Andrew Irvine left camp and headed for the **summit**. They were using a new tool, **oxygen** in bottles, to help them breathe. But they never came back.

oxygen bottle

George Mallory

DID YOU KNOW?

When asked why he wanted to climb Mount Everest, Mallory said, "Because it is there."

No one knows if Mallory and Irvine reached the **summit**. In 1999, Mallory's body was found lower down the mountain. The mystery is still unsolved.

DID YOU KNOW?

Mallory had a camera, which has never been found. Could it hold a photo of the summit?

Was Mallory the first person to see a view from the summit?

Mallory had a camera like this.

Success at Last

No one had gotten to the top of Mount Everest by 1953. On May 29, Edmund Hillary and Tenzing Norgay were almost there. There was a 40-foot wall of rock between them and the **summit**. Was this the end of their climb?

DID YOU KNOW?

Today, there are ropes in place to help climbers up the rock wall. It is called the Hillary Step.

Norgay stands on the **summit**.

Hillary found a **vertical** crack at the edge of the wall. He wedged himself in and pulled himself up. Then he helped Norgay. After a little more climbing, the two men were standing on top of the world!

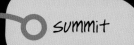

summit

Hillary and
Norgay's route
to the top of
Mount Everest
is shown in red.

Base Camp

W

Climbing

In 1978, Reinhold Messner and Peter Habeler climbed Mount Everest without using bottled **oxygen**. They thought that using bottled oxygen was cheating! Climbing without it meant they had to stop every few steps to catch their breath.

Messner points to the **summit** of Everest on a photograph.

goggles

DID YOU KNOW?

When sunlight bounces off snow, it can cause snow blindness. Climbers wear goggles to protect their eyes.

Super Sherpas

The Sherpa people live in the area around Mount Everest. They often work as mountain guides. Many climbers are amazed at how well the Sherpas cope with **altitude**.

DID YOU KNOW?

Apa Sherpa holds the record for climbing Mount Everest the most times. In 2011, he climbed it for the 21st time!

Crazy Descents

In 2000, Davorin Karničar skied from the **summit** back to the **Base Camp**. Climbing up had taken several days. Skiing down took just five hours! He has skied down mountains on all seven **continents**.

Yuichiro Miura chose to ski down Everest in 1970.

DID YOU KNOW?
Other climbers have snowboarded down Everest. Two even slid down on their bottoms!

Mount Everest by Bike

Most climbers fly to Nepal. In 1996, Göran Kropp rode his bike—from Sweden! It took five months. He climbed Mount Everest alone, came down, and cycled back to Sweden.

Kropp

DID YOU KNOW?
Kropp packed only one set of underwear for the entire trip!

Mount Everest Today

Hundreds of climbers visit Mount Everest each year. That means a lot of litter. There are no garbage cans, so what is left behind stays there—even dead bodies.

People are working to clean up Mount Everest.

Climbers spend several weeks at Base Camp getting used to the altitude.

Timeline

1924 George Mallory and Andrew Irvine disappear on Mount Everest.

1953 Edmund Hillary and Tenzing Norgay are the first to reach the **summit**.

1978 Reinhold Messner and Peter Habeler climb Mount Everest without bottled **oxygen**.

1980 Messner climbs Everest without oxygen again, this time by himself.

1996 Göran Kropp cycles to Mount Everest and back.

1999 Mallory's body is found near the summit.

2000 Davorin Karničar skis down Mount Everest.

2011 Apa Sherpa climbs Mount Everest for the 21st time.

Explorer's Checklist

If you want to climb a mountain, you will need the right gear:

Climbing suit: Like wearing a comforter!

Gloves: A thin inner pair and thick mittens to cover them

Goggles: To protect your eyes from snow blindness

Crampons: For gripping the ice

Oxygen: For breathing— unless you think that's cheating!

Ice ax: For cutting steps into snow—and gripping if you start to fall!

Boots: Must be light but sturdy, warm, and waterproof

Glossary

altitude height above sea level. It is hard to breathe at high altitude, since there is very little oxygen.

Base Camp place where climbers stay before climbing Mount Everest

continent very large land mass. There are seven continents on Earth.

crampon metal plate with spikes fixed to a boot, used for climbing on ice or rock

oxygen gas in the air. We need oxygen to breathe.

sturdy strong and well-built

summit top or highest point of a mountain

vertical straight up and down

Find Out More

Books

Hurley, Michael. *The World's Most Amazing Mountains* (Landform Top Tens). Chicago: Raintree, 2009.

Katz, Jill. *Mount Everest* (Natural Wonders of the World). Mankato, Minn.: Creative Education, 2004.

Mason, Paul. *Mountains Under Threat* (World in Peril). Chicago: Heinemann, 2010.

Websites

kids.nationalgeographic.com/kids/games/ geographygames/quizyournoodle-mount- everest/
Take a quiz about Mount Everest.

kids.nationalgeographic.com/kids/stories/ peopleplaces/sherpa/
Find out lots of information about Sherpas.

Index

altitude 20, 27
Apa Sherpa 21

Base Camp 22, 27
birds 7
breathing 6, 10, 18

cameras 12, 13
climbers 6, 8–27
climbing gear 29
crampons 9, 29
cycling 24

deaths 8, 12

guides 20

Habeler, Peter 18
Hillary, Edmund 14,
   16–17

ice axes 9, 29
Irvine, Andrew 10, 12

Karničar, Davorin 22
Kropp, Göran 24–25

litter 26

Mallory, George
   10–13
map 5
Messner, Reinhold 18

Norgay, Tenzing 14,
   16–17

oxygen 6, 10, 18, 29

Sherpas 20–21
skiing 22
snow blindness 19
snowboarding 23
summit 10, 12, 14,
   17, 18